Bugs and Bugsicles

Insects in the Winter

Amy S. Hansen

Illustrations by Robert C. Kray

BOYDS MILLS PRESS
Honesdale, Pennsylvania

I**T IS LATE** S**EPTEMBER** and the sun is still warm when a Monarch Butterfly lands on a purple aster. She's grabbing a quick sip of nectar before flying south.

A Honeybee aims for a yellow marigold. She will need food to get through the winter.

On the grass below, five Pavement Ants hurry past, carrying seeds. They march underground, going down to their nest to get away from the dangers of frost.

THE RIVERBANK LOOKS EMPTY

without the Dragonfly that usually swoops and plays on the breezes. He has already died, but his young wait safely in the warm mud.

No one notices a Ladybug crawling into his winter home or a Praying Mantis looking for a safe place for her eggs.

A Field Cricket still calls *chirp-CHIRP-CHIRRRRP*. But his concerts are getting shorter as the temperature grows colder.

FARTHER NORTH,

winter is already underway, and the Arctic Woolly Bear Caterpillar is frozen solid. She'll stay that way, safe if not warm, until the spring thaw lets her move again.

In any place that winter touches, the insects pay attention and get ready. The insects that buzz and chirp all summer are quieter in fall. They can't fly as easily. They need the sun's warmth to help heat their bodies. They can't find food. Most need protection from the cold and protection from freezing. Their bodies are made up of tiny cells that hold water. If water freezes inside the cells, it will expand, bursting the cells and killing the insects.

So as the days grow shorter and cooler, insects get ready. Some hide. Some fly away. Others make their own homes, or they warm up the homes they have. And still others lay eggs because eggs will last through the winter even when adults cannot.

Praying Mantis

IT'S EARLY EVENING NOW, time for
Praying Mantis to lay eggs. She doesn't know winter.
She was an egg the last time the winds blew cold and
harsh. She won't live to see this winter either, but her eggs
will. And right now she is flying to a bouquet of birch
trees, a place out of the wind where she can put her eggs.

Squeak, squeak, squeak!

She hears a bat hunting. Praying Mantis drops down, spiraling quickly to the ground. She lands safely, but she's still far away from where she wants to lay her eggs. She needs to hurry. She has many eggs to lay, and winter is coming.

Her triangular head turns, looking left, then right. Finally she sees a clump of rosebushes. They will do. She climbs up and gets started. Carefully she puts one hundred, two hundred, three hundred eggs into her sticky, foamy egg sack. When the sack hardens, it feels like cardboard, but it's strong enough to keep away other insects that might eat the eggs. It will also protect the eggs from the rain and cold.

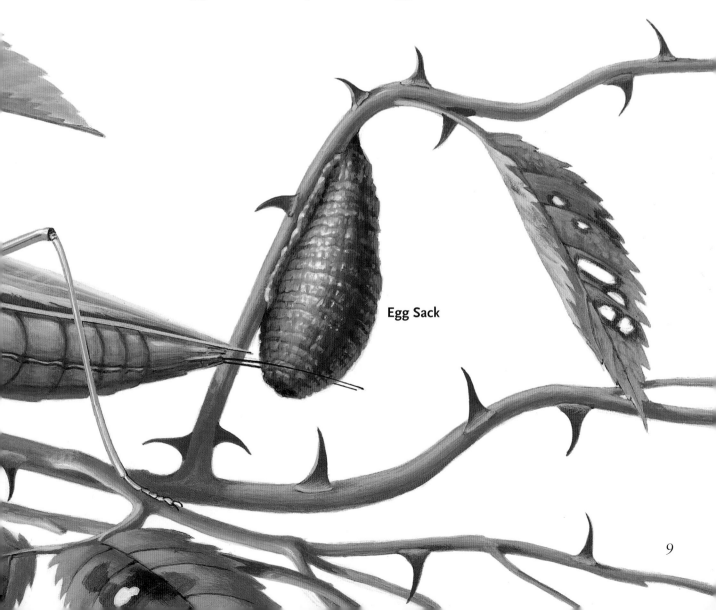

Egg Sack

Field Cricket

TONIGHT, FIELD CRICKET'S SONG
sounds scattered. In the summer he called *chirp-chirp-chirp*.
Now he calls once and waits. It's getting colder. Soon he
won't make a sound at all. He rubs his wings together once
again. *Chirrrrp*. He's hoping to find one more mate this
season. Soon his mates will lay eggs.

The moon rises. Field Cricket rests his wings on his long
back. He spots one of his mates in the dirt. She is poking
holes in the ground with the special digging tool
on her bottom. She lays an egg in each hole and then
quickly buries it.

She is tired, but she needs to finish tonight. Frost is coming. If the ground freezes, she won't be able to dig the holes for her eggs. As the moon sets, she finishes. All four hundred eggs are safely underground.

She flies close to Field Cricket in the grass. They won't live to see their eggs hatch, but the eggs are protected. On the outside, the dirt will keep them from blowing away. And on the inside, an antifreeze called glycerol will keep them soft all winter. Come spring, hundreds of baby crickets will climb out of the dirt, looking like tiny versions of Field Cricket and his mate.

Dragonfly

DRAGONFLY IS NOT YET an adult. He still lives underwater in the young, or nymph, stage. He feels the stream around him chill as the sun goes down. He takes one last bite of worm and leaves the stream for his winter home. He doesn't get out of the water—he goes underneath it.

Splosh. He settles into the warm mud at the bottom of the stream. It's a bubbly nest, warmed by the decaying plants in the streambed.

Breathing underwater is no problem. Dragonfly still has gills like a fish. He needs to stay wet until he changes into a full-grown dragonfly with wings.

Last spring, this dragonfly nymph was an egg. He hatched in the water and wriggled down to the bottom, feeling the stream's gentle current on his light body. Now he is bigger. He waits in the plants for his food to come close, then—*snap!*—his big jaws close over a worm. Sometimes he catches tadpoles and even small fish. Dragonfly is always hungry, and the stream has a constant flow of food. But he needs to be ready to hide, too, because bigger fish would love to have him for lunch.

He won't have to worry during winter, though. He'll stay curled up in the mud.

Not many animals go hunting in the winter. And the mud isn't likely to freeze. This is a time of rest.

In spring, Dragonfly will dig out and start eating again. This year he might be ready to change into a full-grown dragonfly. Then he'll become the amazing flying machine that can zoom, dive, and spin in midair.

But if he changes into an adult, he won't live through another winter. Before summer is over, he'll find a mate. She'll lay eggs, and from those eggs will come the next generation of dragonflies.

Dragonfly Nymph

Ladybug

LADYBUG NEEDS TO HURRY.
The sun is disappearing and with it the warmth that fills
his body and allows him to fly. Even now with the sun
only half-set, his steps are getting stiff and awkward.
He needs to find a home soon, or he will freeze.

He creeps down the stalk of a late-blooming zinnia
and onto a rock. The rock has a little hollow that blocks
the wind. It might work. But wait, it's wet. If he gets
wet, he will freeze. Ladybug keeps looking.

He forces his stiff wings to make one more flight.
Flap, *flutter*, he falls. Too soon, too fast. He hasn't seen a
place to stay.

Crawling up a stump, he finds a hole and many
other ladybugs inside. Ladybug, the last one from the
garden, joins the others in a slow-moving dance, their
bodies merging into one big red and black bundle. By
staying together, they hold on to just enough warmth
to keep from freezing.

When winter comes for good, they will rest in a
kind of hibernation called diapause. Their breathing
slows. They won't eat or drink. They conserve energy.

In spring, Ladybug and the others will feel the
warm sun again. The cluster will crawl apart, mate,
and lay eggs. The ladybugs probably won't live to see
the summer. However, when the eggs hatch, many new
ladybugs will crawl out. And they will be around to
greet the hot summer sun.

Honeybee

HONEYBEE TAKES A LONG drink of nectar from a goldenrod. *Bzzz.* She flies home.

Some of her sisters will make the nectar into honey and then sip the sweet liquid all winter. Other sisters take care of the eggs and the queen bee. There's no such thing as a single honeybee. All the sisters live and work together. And there are a lot of sisters. This winter there will be twenty-five thousand of them in the colony.

Honeybee flies back to the goldenrod and gets more nectar for honey. When it gets cold, she and her sisters will do what many families do—huddle close, closer, *really close*, until all of those thousands of bees take up only as much room as a soccer ball. Then they'll shiver, keeping themselves warm.

All that shaking takes energy.

Through the winter, the bees eat honey, lots of it. One colony of bees can eat one or two pounds of honey a week.

In spring some of the bees leave in search of new flowers and fresh food. The eggs hatch, and a new set of bees is ready. They'll either join the hive or start a new one and make enough food to fuel their own bee cluster next winter.

Pavement Ant

PAVEMENT ANT CAN'T IMAGINE life without other ants. They all work together, especially tonight as winter approaches. Ant and four of her sisters carry a few seeds into the underground nest. Like the honeybees, they have a big household—sisters and sisters and more sisters plus a few brothers and a queen, who lays the eggs.

Crunch. Pavement Ant grabs a bite of apple. Then she marches on with her seed, taking it deep into the underground nest. She goes deeper than they go in the summer. She and her sisters are ready to spend the winter living underground.

Of course, Pavement Ant lives underground in the summer, too. Her home is a maze of tunnels and rooms. There is a room for the eggs, a room for food, and even a place where they go to the bathroom.

In the winter, Pavement Ant and her sisters stop using the rooms at the top of their home. They move deeper into the nest, away from the surface. Down below, the ground rarely freezes. And the ants move together. Pavement Ant's next job is to help carry the nest's precious eggs to the warmest room of the nest. Then she can sleep with her sisters in the not-too-cold earth. In the spring, she'll be ready to help feed the baby ants and to look for more food.

Monarch Butterfly

MONARCH BUTTERFLY lands on a purple aster for another drink. She doesn't like northern winters. She's headed south to Mexico, an incredible journey for a creature no heavier than a paper clip.

The distance isn't the only amazing part. Monarch Butterfly is going to the same spot as the monarchs went last year. But she hadn't hatched when the trip took place last fall. How will she know how to get there? No one knows.

When Monarch Butterfly stops, she will be at a forest on a mountain. The forest is just warm enough to keep her from freezing, and it is dry. In the spring and summer, the cloud forest gets rain almost every day, but in the winter it rarely rains.

Monarch Butterfly will join thousands of other monarchs on the pine trees. They'll hold still and stay together, resting for their next trip. In spring, Monarch Butterfly will be ready to mate and start the long trip north. She will not make it all the way north, but her offspring will.

As Monarch flies over Alabama, she'll see milkweed plants. That's where she'll put her eggs. Monarchs always use milkweed plants, in Texas and in Maine and many other states as well. When Monarch Butterfly dies after laying all her eggs, her young will grow up and be ready to fly. The first group will fly north, live a few weeks, and lay eggs on more milkweed. Then their young will hatch, and the new butterflies will do the same—move north and lay eggs on more milkweed. Their young will do the same. When the "great-great-grandchildren" of that Monarch from Mexico become adults, it will be time for the Monarchs to fly back south, time to spend the winter in Mexico.

Arctic Woolly Bear Caterpillar

FREEZINGWEATHERDOESN'TBOTHER the Arctic Woolly Bear Caterpillar. She lives where temperatures often drop to 40 below zero. She doesn't fight it; she becomes a bugsicle.

For most of her life, she eats like crazy during the short Arctic spring and summer. She munches the gray-green Arctic willow leaves and bright purple saxifrage flowers. And then she lies and wiggles in the sunlight, taking the sun's energy

into her fuzzy body, feeling the warmth in her eight pink hind feet.

By mid-July, the weather is a little cooler and it's time to get ready for winter. She stops eating and finds a rock where she will spin her winter cocoon. But even as she finishes and goes to sleep, her body is hard at work. She's getting ready to perform an amazing trick. She will freeze in the winter, thaw out in the spring, and start all over.

Woolly Bear won't need to breathe while she's frozen. She isn't dead. She isn't really asleep. She's a bugsicle.

WINTER IS HERE. The insects are ready. Some are hiding, some have laid eggs, and some flew away. Some will work hard at staying warm, while others simply freeze. Each bug has a way of surviving until spring.

THEN, WHEN THE GROUND WARMS

and the air is soft with rain, they'll come out again. They'll eat and grow all summer until the air grows cold and it is once again time to be a winter bug—or maybe a bugsicle.

Adult Dragonfly

27

Author's Note

When I was young, bugs seemed magical. They'd be buzzing around all summer, and then as it got cold, they'd disappear. Where did they go? And how did they get back to my yard in the spring? Years later my kids asked the same questions, and I decided to find out.

This book shows insects that hide, insects that fly away, and insects that lay eggs. Of course, there are more strategies to get through the winter than can fit in this book. But these strategies are also used by many common insects. Grasshoppers, for example, lay eggs just as their cricket cousins do. Spruce beetles hide from the cold, living under the top layer of spruce trees' bark, just as the dragonfly nymph uses mud. Mosquitoes, on the other hand, cover all their bases, laying eggs and crawling into the bark of trees, so in spring there are two generations alive and biting.

What really fascinated me, though, were the insects that freeze. Actually, the freezing by itself isn't that impressive. What is amazing is that they thaw out—going from bug to bugsicle and back again. Most animals could not survive freezing. If the water in your body froze, it would expand, bursting all of its containers, such as veins, arteries, and major organs.

The Arctic Woolly Bear Caterpillar has two main protection systems. First, the woolly bear has antifreeze—different from the poisonous antifreeze used in cars. The chemicals keep the bug from freezing too early. They also coat the cell walls, making it harder for ice to get to them.

Second, the woolly bear uses special bacteria to create ice-starters in its abdomen. So when it's time to freeze, the ice has something to grab on to. This forces the ice to start in the gut and then move out to the veins. As the ice forms, it pulls water out of the nearby cells, so those cells are dehydrated and ice crystals won't grow inside them.

In the spring, the bug thaws out, seemingly unfazed by the winter's cold. For at least seven years, the Arctic Woolly Bear Caterpillar does this freeze-thaw routine until it's mature enough to become a moth.

That's one cool life cycle!

Adult Woolly Bear Moth

Frozen Solid

What happens when water freezes?
Check out your predictions with this experiment.

What You Need
- Water
- 2 drinking cups
- 2 or more clear plastic drinking straws
- Play-Doh
- 2 different-colored marking pens

What to Do
1. Practice using a straw to pick up water. Fill one cup about halfway with water. Place a straw in the water. Then put your finger over the top hole. When you lift the straw out of the water, keep your finger over the hole and the water will stay in place. Move your finger off the hole, and the water runs out.
2. When you are good at picking up water, fill your straw about halfway. Plug the bottom with a large lump of Play-Doh.
3. Mark the level of the water using a pen.
4. Use a pen of another color to mark where you think the ice will be when the water is frozen.
5. Put the straw upright in the empty cup.
6. Repeat steps 2 through 5 with another straw so you have two straws filled halfway with water. (The second straw is a backup, in case the first plug leaks.)
7. Place both water-filled straws in the freezer. Check after ten minutes and again after twenty. How close were your predictions?

What Happened?
The water, or ice, should have moved higher, reaching above the first pen mark. Water is unusual. When it freezes, it expands by 4 percent of its original size. Because water expands, ice is actually less dense than liquid water, so it floats. This is why animals can live in ponds year-round, even in places that get cold. The ice floats on top of the pond, insulating the water from the really cold air and keeping the snow and ice out of the water. Fish and insects such as dragonfly nymphs never feel the cold winds blow.

Will It Freeze?

Remember how some insects slow down the freezing process?
They use antifreeze. If you ride in a car in the winter, it probably has antifreeze in it.
The antifreeze used in cars is a poisonous mixture that includes salt and sugar and water.
Insects' antifreeze comes from glycerol, the smooth, shiny stuff in soap bubbles.
You can create your own antifreeze.

What You Need

Marking pen •

4 plastic drinking cups •

Measuring cup •

Warm water •

Measuring spoons •

Salt •

What to Do

1. Use the marking pen to label the cups *W*, *1SW*, *2SW*, and *3SW*.
2. Pour a 1/2 cup of warm water into each cup.
3. Leave the first cup as plain water.
4. Add 1 tablespoon of salt to the cup labeled *1SW*. Stir until the salt dissolves.
5. Add 2 tablespoons of salt to the cup labeled *2SW*. Stir until the salt dissolves.
6. Add 3 tablespoons of salt to the cup labeled *3SW*. Stir until the salt dissolves.
7. Put the cups in the freezer.
8. Check them every half hour.

Which one freezes first? Which one freezes last? If some don't freeze, what is their consistency—are they thick and syrupy or thin and watery?

What Happened?

The plain water will freeze first, at a temperature of 32 degrees Fahrenheit (0 degrees Celsius). Because salt lowers the freezing point of water, the others will freeze more slowly. The water with the most salt will freeze last.

To my bugs: B.C., S.C., and E.C. And to Andy who saw this book through

—A.H.

To my wife, Jackie, and my two sons,
Bob II and Bruce

—R.C.K.

Acknowledgments

For their generous help in reviewing the text and illustrations for this book, I thank Dr. Richard E. Lee, Miami University, Oxford, Ohio; Gary Parsons, Michigan State University; Dr. Hugh Danks, Canadian Museum of Nature, Ottawa, Ontario, Canada; Kenneth Lorenzen, University of California, Davis; Dr. Beth Norden, honeybee expert, Greenbelt, Maryland; Butch (Arnold) Norden, Maryland Department of Natural Resources; and Dr. Olga Kukal, Atlantic Low Temperature Systems, Ltd., Halifax, Nova Scotia, Canada.

For their invaluable assistance in helping with specific issues, I thank Dr. David Gray, California State University, Northridge; Paul van Westendorp, P.Ag., British Columbia Ministry of Agriculture, Food, and Fisheries, Abbotsford, British Columbia, Canada; and Dr. Yves Le Conte, Laboratoire Biologie et Protection de l'Abeille, Saint-Paul, France.

Text copyright © 2010 by Amy S. Hansen
Illustrations copyright © 2010 by Robert C. Kray
Photographs by Stanton Pratt, © 2010 by Boyds Mills Press
All rights reserved

Boyds Mills Press, Inc.
815 Church Street
Honesdale, Pennsylvania 18431
Printed in China

Library of Congress Cataloging-in-Publication Data

Hansen, Amy.
  Bugs and bugsicles : insects in the winter / Amy S. Hansen ; illustrations by Robert C. Kray. — 1st ed.
       p. cm.
  Includes bibliographical references and index.
  ISBN 978-1-59078-269-9 (hardcover : alk. paper)
  ISBN 978-1-59078-763-2 (paperback)
  1. Insects—Wintering—Juvenile literature. 2. Insects—Behavior—Juvenile literature. 3. Insects—Ecology—Juvenile literature. I. Kray, Robert Clement. II. Title.
  QL496.H36 2010
  595.714'3—dc22

                          2009024073
First edition
First Boyds Mills Press paperback edition, 2010
The text of this book is set in 13-point Sabon.
The illustrations are done in acrylic.

10 9 8 7 6 5 4 3 2 1 (HC)
10 9 8 7 6 5 4 3 2 1 (PB)

Additional Reading

Books
Bright Beetle
Rick Chrustowski
Illustrations by the author
Henry Holt, 2000. Ages 4 to 8

Chirp, Chirp! Crickets in Your Backyard
Nancy Loewen
Illustrations by Rick Peterson
Picture Window Books, 2006. Ages 4 to 8

Web Sites*
Smithsonian National Museum of Natural History Department of Entomology
entomology.si.edu

California Academy of Sciences Library. "Kids' Insect Bibliography."
www.calacademy.org/research/library/biodiv/biblio/kidbugs.htm

Glossary

antifreeze a substance that, when added to water, lowers water's freezing point.

diapause a time of rest for insects, similar to hibernation in other animals.

glycerol a thick liquid made of a sugary alcohol. It is sometimes found in antifreeze.

ice-starter bacteria (or other substance) that gives water something to hold on to as the water turns to ice.

Index

*Active at time of publication